my first
magic book

my first magic book

50 fun tricks and illusions for children aged 7 years +

Paul Megram

CICO **kidz**

Published in 2014 by CICO Kidz
An imprint of Ryland Peters & Small
519 Broadway, 5th Floor, New York NY 10012
20–21 Jockey's Fields, London WC1R 4BW

www.rylandpeters.com

10 9 8 7 6 5 4 3 2 1

ISBN: 978-1-78249-158-3

Printed in China

Series consultant: Susan Akass
Editors: Susan Akass and Clare Sayer
Designer: Barbara Zuñiga
Photographer: Penny Wincer
Stylist: Isabel de Cordova
Animal artworks: Hannah George
Step artworks: Rachel Boulton

Contents

Introduction

There is nothing quite like magic to amaze and amuse your friends. **My First Magic Book** gives you step-by-step instructions for tricks that you can perform almost immediately. Some of them are the kind of illusion you could perform in a magic show, others are fun tricks that will make your friends groan at having been caught out so easily.

To help you find your way around, **My First Magic Book** has been divided into six chapters, each one showing you how to do a different kind of trick.

1 Card Tricks. These tricks, with a simple deck of playing cards, could be part of a magic show. They will get your friends looking in amazement and saying, "How did you do that?"

2 Tricks with Everyday Objects. This section shows you that you can make magic with the kinds of bits and pieces that you find around the house. No need for expensive props—things like paperclips, paper napkins, and hair elastics will do the trick!

3 Puzzlers & Betchas. The puzzles here will really get those heads scratching. They are simple but effective brainteasers to entertain your friends and family. Plus, how many times have you said to friends or your parents, "Betcha can't do this?" These tricks will make sure that you always win the bet!

4 Money Tricks. All magicians do clever things with money! Get yourself a banknote and some coins, and learn the money tricks in this chapter. These are definitely tricks to add to your show.

5 Mind Tricks. Have you ever wanted to read someone's mind? Do these tricks well and your audience will believe that you really can see what they are thinking.

6 Pranks. Who doesn't enjoy playing a practical joke on a friend? These tricks will have your friends squirming with disgust and groaning with disbelief. Watch out everyone—here you come!

All the tricks in this book are easy, but some need more practice than others. We have graded them with one or two smiley faces to help you know which is which. You could do the level one tricks almost immediately. The level two tricks need quicker fingers and some convincing acting skills, so you should practice and practice in front of the mirror before you try them on your friends. Remember though, magic tricks are best kept a secret. Go out and have fun making magic, but keep the ideas from this book under your (magic) hat!

Magician's Props

Why not find yourself a box or case in which you can put all your magician's props?
You could decorate it with magical symbols such as moons and stars to make it mysterious.
Add the props you need to your case as you learn to do each new trick.
Here is a list of the props used for the tricks in this book. They are all very basic items
that you will find around your house:

A full deck of cards

An old deck of cards (it doesn't matter if there are a few missing)

Some coins

A clothespin (peg)

Elastic bands or hair elastics

Paper napkins (cheap, thin ones are best!)

A banknote (a foreign or a play one is fine)

Transparent plastic cups

Paper cups

White card

Paper

Scissors

Pen

Pencil

Colored pens

Wax crayons

Glue stick

Paperclips

A colorful cloth or scarf—silk ones look very professional

Matchboxes

A pile of spent matches (ask an adult to light them for you and then blow them out quickly, or buy craft sticks from craft stores)

Candies (sweets)—these will need replacing regularly!

A hat

Lengths of rope or thick cord

Sheets of newspaper

A spool of thread (reel of cotton)

A needle

Your Costume

If you are aiming to put on a magic show at a party or to entertain friends or relations, it is fun to look the part. Wear something out of the ordinary—perhaps a long cloak or a special hat! You might also like to make and use a magic wand, which you could use in tricks such as the "Vanishing Coin" on page 76.

Your Spiel

A spiel is what you say while doing your tricks. The more you say and the more confidently you say it, the less likely it is that your audience will notice how you are tricking them. Try to watch some magicians on TV and copy the way they talk. Begin your tricks with words like "Ladies and gentlemen, boys and girls, you see before you a perfectly ordinary pack of cards…" Practice your spiel until you are really good at it.

Trick levels

Level 1
These are short, easy illusions that beginners should start with.

Level 2
You will need a bit of practice with these tricks, but they are still quite easy.

Level 3
These are more challenging illusions that you can try if you have mastered some of the easier tricks.

chapter 1
Card Tricks

The Four Robbers

Part of this trick is about telling a good "story"—so that your audience is distracted and doesn't see how you do it!

The preparation

You will need

A deck of cards

1 Take three random cards from the deck, as well as the four jacks.

2 Place the four jacks on top of the three cards. Pull them together into a neat pile so that the random cards are hidden from view beneath the jacks. In this way, the audience only see the jacks.

The trick

1 Place the deck of cards face down on the table. Tell your audience that you have taken out the four jacks. Show them the four jacks very carefully, keeping the random cards underneath hidden. Then place all seven cards (your audience must believe there are only four) face down on top of the rest of the deck of cards. Hold the cards at an angle as you put them down so your audience can see a jack at the bottom. Tell them: "The four jacks are robbers and are about to rob the bank. The bank they want to rob is the rest of the deck of cards."

2 Next you are going to move the three random cards (which are now at the top) to positions lower down the deck (or bank as it is now called in this trick). Take the top card and, without showing it, say: "The first robber walks in through the front door of the bank." Place this card near the bottom of the deck.

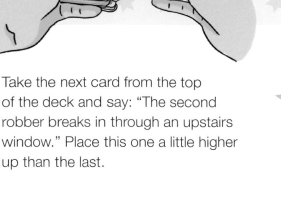

3 Take the next card from the top of the deck and say: "The second robber breaks in through an upstairs window." Place this one a little higher up than the last.

4 Take the third card from the top, and say: "The third robber climbs in through the skylight." This time place the card near to the top of the deck.

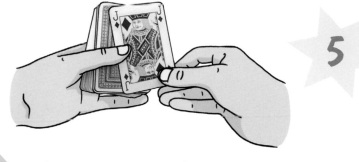

5 Now say: "The fourth robber stays on the roof as the lookout." Turn the top card over, revealing one of the jacks, before turning it face down again.

6 Continue with the story by saying: "At 3 o'clock in the morning, the robbers meet back up on the roof with all the stolen money to make their getaway in a waiting helicopter." Tap the deck three times.

How did the SNEAKY bank robbers GET AWAY?

7 Turn the top four cards over to reveal that the four jacks (robbers) have returned to the top of the deck.

The secret

Everybody thinks you moved the three jacks into the middle of the deck, but only you know about the three random cards that you set up at the start—it is these cards that were actually moved.

Amazing Aces

This trick is so simple to do and will wow your audience every time, all you need is a pack of cards. Have fun keeping people guessing how you did it!

The preparation

You will need

A deck of cards

1 Remove all four aces from your deck of cards. Place your deck of cards face down on a table. Place the ace of diamonds face down on top of the deck.

2 Place the other aces (hearts, spades, and clubs) in your hand and arrange them so that the ace of spades is on the top, the ace of hearts is in the middle, and the ace of clubs is behind. When you show them to your audience, the red "A" should be the only thing visible of the red card. The audience should not see that it is a heart card.

The trick

1 Show the cards in your hand to your audience, making sure that they can only see the red "A" of the heart card.

2 Turn the cards face down and slot them into the deck in the following order: the red ace is placed in the middle of the deck, the ace of spades is placed at the top, and the ace of clubs goes at the bottom of the deck.

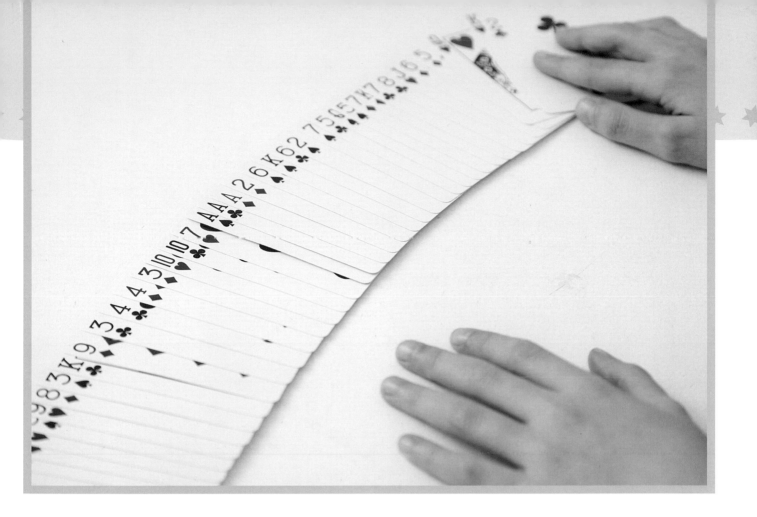

An "ACE" trick!

3 Ask a member of your audience to cut the cards. Take them back and spread them out on the table, facing up. To your audience's surprise, the three aces are still together in the middle of the deck.

The secret

Although it looks as though the ace of diamonds is used and placed in the deck during the trick, the card that you actually place in the deck is the ace of hearts. The heart is hidden by the two black cards (see The preparation, step 2), so the only part of the red card that the audience sees is the red "A."

The ace of diamonds is actually placed on the top of the deck face down, before the trick starts. So when the ace of spades is placed on top of the deck, it sits on top of the ace of diamonds. Cutting the cards brings them all together, as if by magic.

21-Card Trick

This trick works every time—as long as you collect up the cards in the right order. Follow the steps below to amaze your friends again and again!

The trick

1 Deal out 21 cards in three rows. Always make sure you go from left to right, starting at the top and making sure that the cards overlap.

2 Ask a friend to pick a card from the ones laid out in front of you and tell you which row their card is in—row 1, 2, or 3? They shouldn't tell you which card it is.

3 Now pick up all the cards, one row at a time, making sure that whichever row your friend has picked goes into the middle of the pile. So if their card was the ace of spades in row 3, pick up another row first, then pick up row 3, and put it on top, then pick up the final row, and put it on top, sandwiching the chosen row in the middle.

4 Now turn the cards over and deal them again in three rows, making sure that the cards are not mixed up and are dealt from left to right.

5 Ask your friend to look for their original card and tell you which row it is in. Pick up the rows, again putting whichever row they chose in the middle of the other two rows.

6 Repeat steps 3 and 4 one more time and then collect up the cards as before. Now for the magic! Simply deal out 10 cards, face down. Turn over the eleventh card and declare that this is the card your friend was thinking of. They will be amazed!

The secret

This trick is all to do with maths. Maybe you can figure out how it works!

COUNT OUT some magic!

Number Force

In this trick you will be able to make a named card appear by counting a certain number of cards—even though your audience chooses the number of cards to count!

The preparation

You will need

....

A deck of cards

Take a deck of cards in your hand and secretly look at the ninth card before the trick starts. This is the card you are going to "force"—in this case the two of hearts.

The trick

1 Announce to your audience that you are going to find your favorite card (in this case, the two of hearts, or whatever the ninth card in the deck was) to appear. Ask a friend to think of a number between 10 and 20 and name it out loud.

2 Deal the same number of cards as the number they said from the top of the deck, face down.

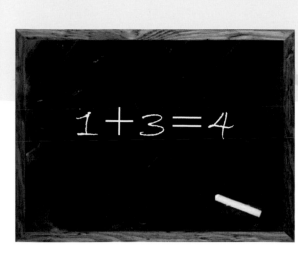

$$1 + 3 = 4$$

3 Next ask them to add the two digits of their chosen number together. So, if they chose the number 13, then they need to add 1 and 3 together.

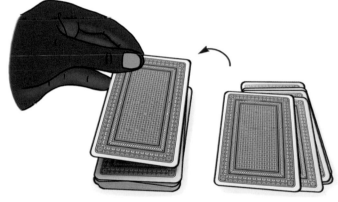

4 Now ask them to place that number of cards back on the deck, in this case four.

5 The card you said you would find will always be the next card.

The secret

You will always be able to find the ninth card because whichever number between 10 and 20 they choose, the math always works. For example, if they choose the number 12, you count out 12 cards, then count back 3 cards (1 + 2), and you get to 9. If they choose 17, you count out 17 cards, then count back 8 cards (1 + 7), and you still get to 9.

MATH Magic!

Ten

You will need to share the secret of this trick with a partner so that you can show off your "mind-reading" skills.

The preparation

You will need

....

A deck of cards

A partner

Find the ten of diamonds in your deck of cards and make sure it is close to the top of the deck.

The trick

1 Lay out the top 10 cards of the deck (which must include the ten of diamonds) in front of you, arranging them in three rows like this:

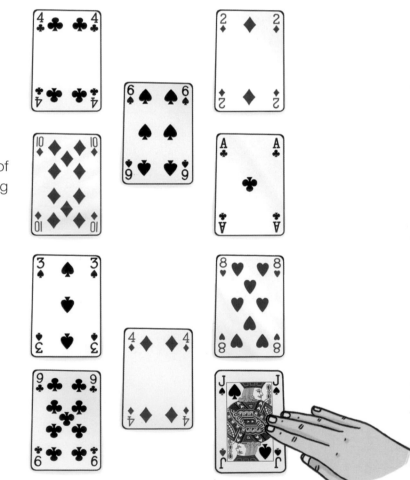

2 Ask your partner to leave the room (or to close their eyes). Ask one of the audience to point to a card.

3 Ask your partner to come back into the room (or open their eyes), and then announce that you are going to read each other's minds to pick the chosen card. Have a bit of fun staring deeply into each other's eyes, pretending that you are mind-reading.

4 Point to any of the cards (except the correct one or the ten of diamonds) and ask your partner to say whether it is the chosen card. The answer will be "No."

5 Now point to the ten of diamonds, This is the clever part of the trick. If you look at the way the cards are laid out, you will see that they match the pattern of diamond shapes on the ten of diamonds. So, when you point to the ten of diamonds, place your finger on the diamond that matches the position of the chosen card (in this case the second diamond down in the left-hand row). Now your partner knows which is the correct card (in this case the ace of clubs). When you point to the correct card, they will immediately answer "Yes!" (Remember, if the chosen card is the ten of diamonds the same rule applies: point to the correct diamond and your partner will know immediately!)

I can READ your mind!

The secret

The important thing is to agree with your partner that you will always point to a "wrong" card first, but when you point to the ten of diamonds, this will let them know which card was chosen. Have fun!

Peg It

This trick will have your friends scratching their heads in puzzlement—why can't they pin the clothespin on the queen?

The preparation

You will need

....

An old deck of cards

Glue stick

Clothespin (peg) or paperclip

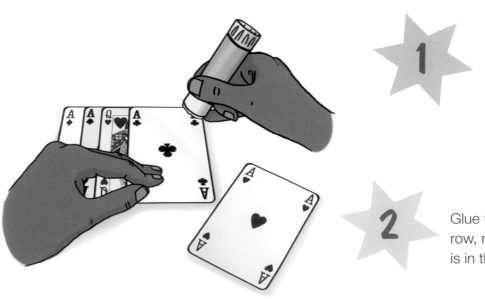

1 Remove the four aces and a queen from the deck of cards.

2 Glue the five cards together in a row, making sure that the queen is in the middle of the row.

The trick

1 Now you are ready to perform. Show the row of glued cards to your friends and ask them to memorize the cards (which seems really easy). Turn the cards face down and then ask a volunteer to attach a clothespin to the queen.

2 Now turn over the cards. The clothespin will always be in the wrong place!

A real head SCRATCHER!

The secret

Because of the way the cards are glued together, from the back it looks as though the clothespin is going over the middle card, when it is actually going over one of the aces.

Card Catch

The trick here is not to let your audience look too closely at the two cards you place in the middle of the deck.

The preparation

You will need
....

A deck of cards

Take a deck of cards. Remove the six of spades and the eight of clubs and put them to one side. Now take out the six of clubs and place it on top of the deck. Take out the eight of spades and place it at the bottom of the deck.

The trick

1 Put the eight of clubs and six of spades face down on the table beside the deck. Pick them up and show them briefly to your audience, saying confidently "Here are the six of clubs and the eight of spades." Your audience won't notice that you are actually holding the six of spades and the eight of clubs.

2 Place the two cards somewhere in the middle of the deck and then square up the deck.

3 Now toss the pack from one hand to the other. Squeeze the top and bottom cards between the fingers and thumb of your throwing hand so you keep hold of them, but let all the cards in between slip out. This needs some practice! If you can catch the falling cards in your other hand it looks impressive, but the trick is just as good if they fall to the floor!

Magical JUMPING cards!

4 Turn over the two cards left in your hand. Your audience will be amazed as those same cards that you placed in the middle of the pack have now jumped out—as if by magic!

A Lucky Guess

This is a simple trick; it's very easy to impress your friends with your mind-reading skills!

The preparation

Make a mental note of the card at the bottom of the deck, in this case the ace of diamonds.

The trick

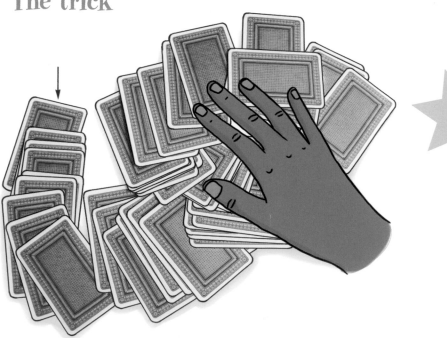

⬟ **1**

Spread the deck of cards face down on a table, in what looks like a random order. You can shuffle them around a little, as long as you remember where the bottom card is.

2 Ask a volunteer to "find" the ace of diamonds (or whatever card was at the bottom of your deck) by pointing to any card they choose. Pick up their chosen card and take a look at it, making sure that no one else can see its value. Even though they won't have got it right, pretend they have, look amazed, and congratulate them on finding the correct card.

3 Now say that you can do just as well as they did—you will point to a card in the deck and will be able to name it correctly. However, when you point, point to the card that was the bottom card of the deck (the ace of diamonds) but name the card that the volunteer has just chosen (in this case the five of hearts). Pick up the ace of diamonds and put it with the card that the volunteer chose.

4 Turn over both the cards together. The audience will be amazed to see that both guesses were correct. (They will have no idea in which order you picked up the two cards!)

X-RAY eyes!

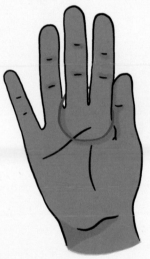

chapter 2
Tricks with everyday objects

Paperclip Wedding

A trick to get your best friends laughing—tell them that you can join two paperclips together without touching them. Give the paperclips the names of a girl and boy in your class who fancy each other, or say that one clip is you and the other is your favorite pop star and now is the time for a wedding!

The preparation

You will need

....

A piece of paper approximately
8 x 2 in. (20 x 5 cm)

2 paperclips

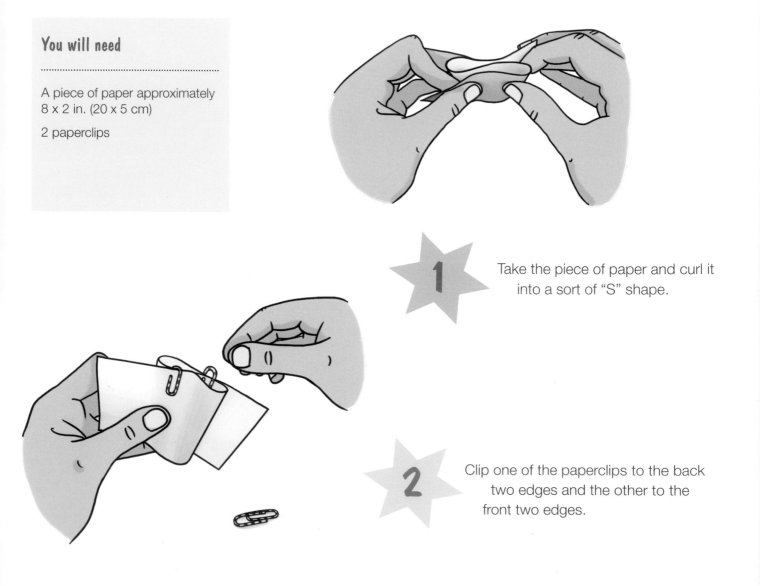

1 Take the piece of paper and curl it into a sort of "S" shape.

2 Clip one of the paperclips to the back two edges and the other to the front two edges.

The trick

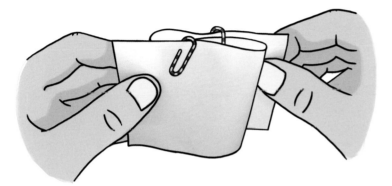

1 Hold the strip of paper at both ends. Ask your friends, "Are you ready for the wedding?" You could even sing the Wedding March. As you sing, pull the two ends apart quickly.

2 The two paperclips will do a triple somersault before linking together as a sign of their undying love.

How do they join TOGETHER?

Knot a Rope

The trick here is not to let your audience see the end of the rope in your hand.

The preparation

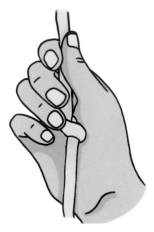

Tie a knot in the end of a piece of rope before the trick starts.

You will need

A length of rope

The trick

1 Hold the rope in one hand so that the knot is tucked inside your hand and hidden from view.

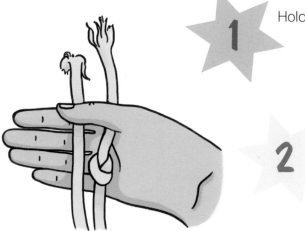

2 Bring the two ends together by putting the unknotted end in your hand, again hiding the knot at the other end from view.

3 Announce that you will magically tie a knot in the rope. With a flick of the wrist, drop the end with the knot in. It will appear that you have somehow managed to tie a knot in the rope at lightning speed.

A KNOTTY problem!

Jumping Bands

The band is clearly seen over two fingers, but with a click of the fingers it jumps to the other two fingers. So how is it done?

The preparation

You will need

A hair elastic, or an elastic band that is about the same size as a hair elastic

1 Before you start, you need to arrange the band over your fingers the right way. With your palm facing you, place the band over your index and middle fingers.

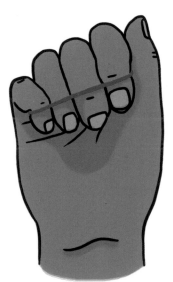

2 Now bend all four fingers down, as if you are gripping something in your hand, and tuck them into the band. Your audience should only be able to see the back of your hand, where it looks as though the band is just tucked around two fingers.

The trick

Show the front of your fingers to your audience and tell them that you will "magically" make the band jump from your first and second fingers to your third and fourth fingers. All you need to do now is slightly open up your fingers and the band will flip from one side to the other. To make the trick more interesting, you could announce that on the count of three you will click the fingers of your other hand and the band will jump at that precise moment.

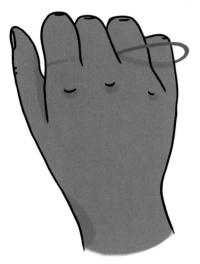

MAGIC fingers!

Napkin Strength Test ☺☺☺

All you need for this amazing feat of strength
is two paper napkins and some good
distraction techniques!

The trick

1 Say to a friend that this is a competition to
see which of you can squeeze a paper
napkin into the smallest ball.

You will need

....

2 identical paper napkins—thin
ones are best

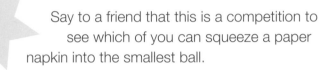

2 Ask your friend to choose one of the
napkins—they are the same, so it
doesn't matter which one they pick.

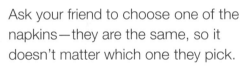

3 Hold your napkin by one corner and
make a fist. Tell your friend to do
the same.

4 But here's the trick. When you put the corner of the napkin into your hand, you secretly break the paper. Although it is now in two pieces, your friend still believes you have just one.

5 Now explain that you need to push the napkin that pokes out at the bottom up into your fist and then repeat with the napkin poking out of the top.

6 While you are explaining how to push the napkin into your fist, rest your hand on the edge of the table and use your other hand to point to their napkin. You need to distract them so much that they won't notice when you let the larger piece of your napkin drop to the floor. (You could put your foot on it to hide it when it has dropped.)

napkin strength test **35**

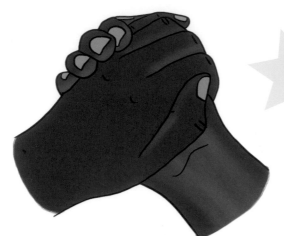

7 Now explain that you both have to hold the paper ball in your hand so nothing can be seen through your fingers, and then you have to squeeze and squeeze to make the ball as small as possible—the smaller they can make their ball, the more chance they have of winning!

8 Your tricky bit is now over. All you have to do is scrunch up and squeeze your ball in the same way as your friend. However, you will have to act a bit here by pretending to have a much larger ball in your hand.

9 After squeezing and on the count of three, you both open up your hands to reveal the winner. Of course, you will win every time!

Your friends will never know you're **CHEATING!**

Banana Split

😊 ◯ ◯

Take a banana, and with magic powers combined with karate skills, you can demonstrate the ancient art of banana splitting.

The preparation

You will need
....

A banana

A pin

A little bit of patience!

1 Take a banana and, following one of the natural seams along its length, push a pin right inside.

2 Push the pin through the banana but not through the skin on the other side. Wiggle it from side to side and pull it out.

3 Repeat step 2 until you have made 10 tiny holes along the banana. Make the holes an equal distance apart.

The trick

1 Tell your audience that you can chop the banana into little pieces inside its skin.

2 Lay the banana on a flat surface and pretend to karate chop it, but hit it quite lightly with the edge of your hand.

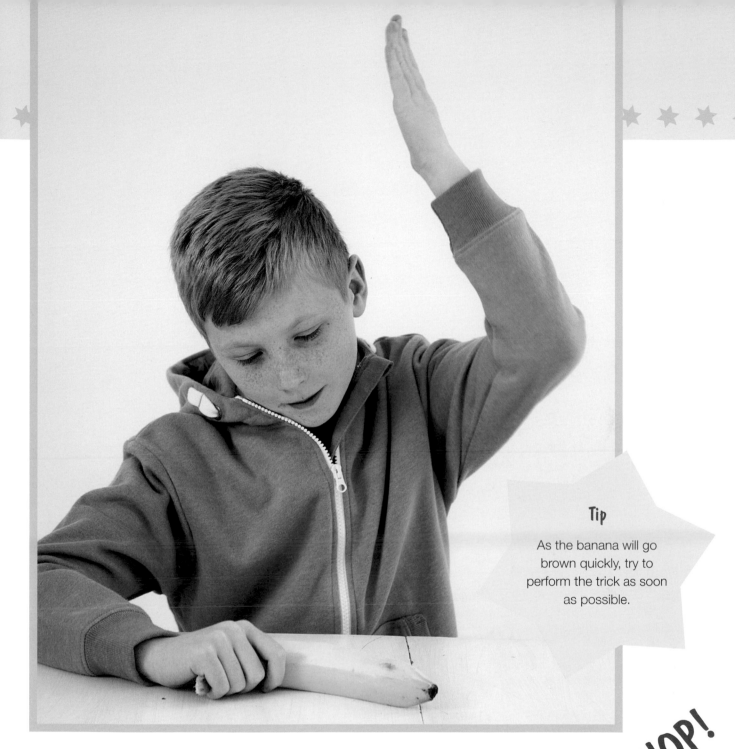

Karate chop, chop, CHOP!

3 Peel the banana. It will be in slices. To end the trick, eat a slice of banana and offer the rest to your audience.

The Jumping Match

Make a match jump! You might need to practice this a few times to make sure you can make it work, but once you've got the hang of it you can show your friends a mini miracle!

The preparation

You will need

··

2 spent (used) long matches

Explain to your friend that when a doctor or nurse takes your pulse, they use two fingers rather than their thumb. This is because your thumb has its own pulse. You are going to show them that this is true.

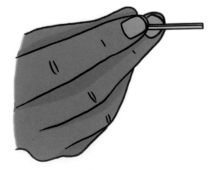

The trick

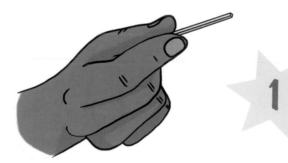

1 Take the first match and hold it between your thumb and first finger.

2 Place your middle finger behind the match. You need to push the finger quite tight up against the match.

3 Now place the second match on top of the first one, using one of your other fingers to help balance it.

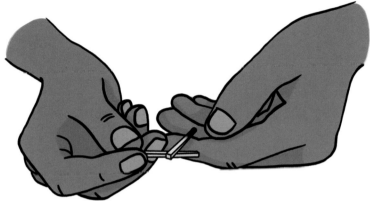

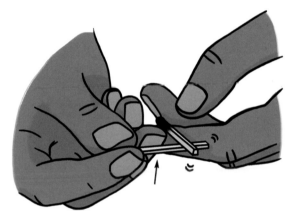

4 Explain that your heartbeat travels from your heart, along your arm, to the thumb where, if you watch closely, it will make the other match jump. Sure enough, within a few seconds the second match does indeed twitch and jump.

All in a HEARTBEAT!

The secret

It's nothing to do with your heart—it's all to do with forces and friction, but they don't really need to know that.

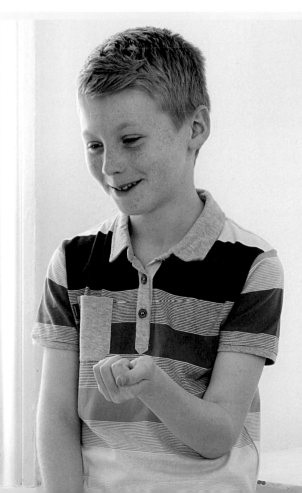

The Rising Ring

With an elastic band, a borrowed ring, and the power of your mind, watch your friends' faces as the ring magically rises in your hands.

The trick

You will need

A thin elastic band

A ring

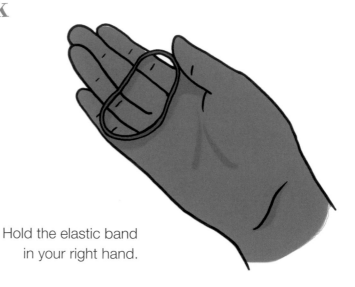

1 Hold the elastic band in your right hand.

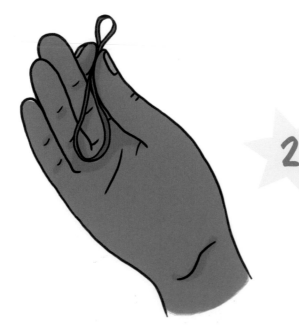

2 Pinch one end of the band with your right finger and thumb to make a loop.

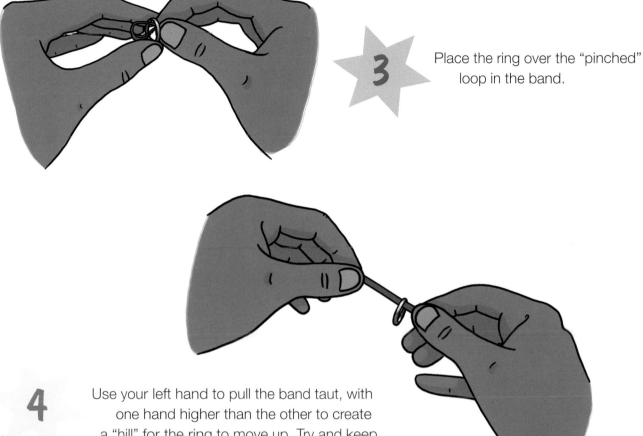

3 Place the ring over the "pinched" loop in the band.

4 Use your left hand to pull the band taut, with one hand higher than the other to create a "hill" for the ring to move up. Try and keep both hands still but slowly release the tension from the elastic band in your right hand and the ring will climb "up the hill."

How does it do THAT?

The secret

As the tension is released from your right hand, the ring stays in the same position on the band. It's the band that is moving, not the ring; the ring just appears to be going upwards.

chapter 3
Puzzlers & betchas

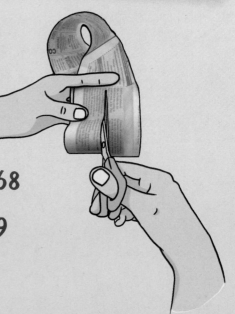

Chicken, Fox, and Corn ☺○○

You could just get your friends to work out how to do this puzzle in their heads, but it's more fun to cut out a chicken, a fox, a bag of corn, and a boat and get your audience to push them back and forth across a "river."

You will need

Paper

Felt-tip pens or crayons

Scissors

2 pencils

The preparation

Simply trace or copy the pictures on the right, color them in, and cut them out.

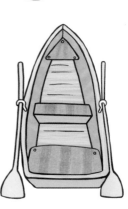

The problem

1 Tell your audience that you need to get a chicken, a fox, and a bag of corn across a river. Mark out a river with a couple of pencils.

2 Tell them that, luckily, you have a boat. Unfortunately, it is so small that it will only carry you and one of the three things you have to carry across, so you'll need to take them across one at a time. But there's a problem! If you take the fox first the chicken will eat the corn, and if you take the corn first the fox will eat the chicken. So how can you get them all across?

The solution

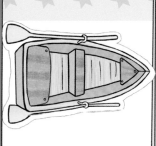

1 First cross the river with the chicken, leaving the fox with the corn. Go back to the fox and the corn.

2 Now take the fox across and leave it on the other side of the river. Go back across the river, but this time take the chicken back with you.

3 Leave the chicken on the left bank and take the corn across the river. Leave the corn with the fox and go back across the river.

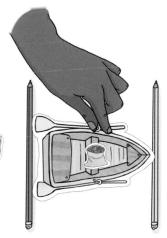

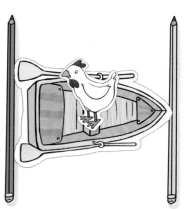

4 Finally, cross the river for the last time with the chicken.

Step-through Paper

How can you step through a piece of letter (A4) paper? Challenge your friends to do it. Give them a piece of paper and a pair of scissors and see what they come up with. Then show them just how easy it is.

You will need

Several sheets of letter (A4) paper

Scissors

The trick

1 Challenge your friends to cut a piece of the paper so they can step through it. Some clever friends may come up with the answer—most will quickly give up.

2 Now show them how to do it. Take a new piece of paper and fold it in half lengthwise.

3 About 1¼ in. (3 cm) from one end, cut from the fold toward the edge of the paper, stopping about 1¼ in. (3 cm) from the edge (it doesn't have to be exact). Make another cut about 2 in. (5 cm) from the first. Make cuts like this all along the paper. The last should be about 1¼ in. (3 cm) from the other end.

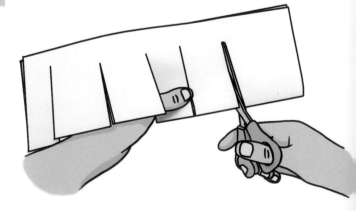

4 Now, starting at the edge, make a cut between the first two cuts you made, cutting towards the fold. Stop about 1¼ in. (3 cm) from the fold. Make another cut between the next two cuts. Keep going like this so that you make a kind of zigzag pattern.

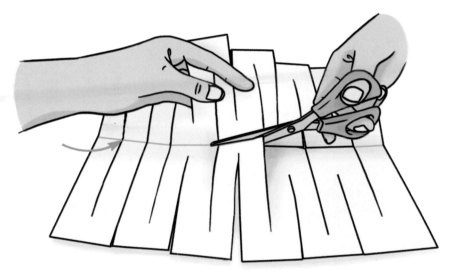

5 Open the paper out. Put your scissors inside the first cut (not at the edge—you don't want to cut the paper in half!) and cut along the fold, finishing at the last cut you made (where the arrow is pointing on the diagram above).

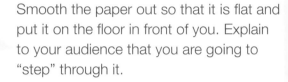

6 Smooth the paper out so that it is flat and put it on the floor in front of you. Explain to your audience that you are going to "step" through it.

7 Pull the ends gently apart until the paper is big enough to step through, and pull it up over your body.

Clever CUTTING!

Rattling Matchbox

☺☺○

Your friends may think they know where the empty matchbox is, but their ears will deceive them! You can get matchsticks for crafting from most craft stores.

The preparation

You will need

3 matchboxes with about 8–10 spent (used) matches or craft matchsticks in each box

1 hair elastic or elastic band

1 empty matchbox

Take one of the full matchboxes and use an elastic band or hair elastic to secure it to the inside of your right arm. Make sure you wear a loose, long-sleeved top so that no one can see the matchbox.

The trick

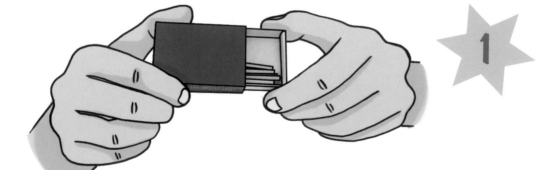

1 Show the three remaining matchboxes (two full, one empty) to your audience. Let them "examine" the matchboxes before you start.

2 Using your left hand (the one without the matchbox on the arm), place the matchboxes on the table in front of you, giving each one a shake as you put it down. Ask your audience to remember where the empty box is and then start to mix them up, still using your left hand. It is important to move them quite slowly — you want everyone to know where the empty one is.

3 Invite someone to point to the empty matchbox. Pick it up and shake it, this time remembering to use your right arm (with the hidden matchbox)! They will have chosen the correct box, but as you shake your arm the secret, hidden matchbox will rattle and "prove" them wrong. You can ask them to have another try, but they will be wrong every time!

Rattle, RATTLE, rattle!

Take 9 Matches

This trick will make your friends groan when you have to tell them the answer because there's nothing magic about it—it's all about thinking in a different way.

The trick

You will need

....

A box of spent (used) matches

1 Give your audience nine matches and ask them to lay them on the table in front of them. Ask them to count them to make sure that there are nine.

2 Now give them two more matches. Tell them to add them to the other matches and still make nine.

3 Watch them scratch their heads for a while and then show them how it's done.

Easy, when you know HOW!

Do as I Do

The rule of the game is to turn two cups over at a time. In three moves (and no fewer), all three cups must be the right way up. Just watch the confusion on your friends' faces!

The trick

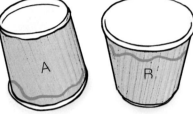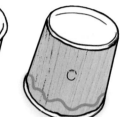

1

Tell your friends that they have to watch you carefully and do what you do. Quickly and confidently set up the cups in the following way, with the middle cup the right way up and the other two facing down.

You will need

....

3 paper cups

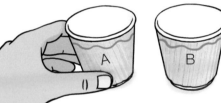

2 Turn the cups over, two at a time, in the following order: A and B, then A and C, then A and B. The cups will now all be the right way up.

3 Now ask one of your friends to do it. Again set out the cups quickly and confidently. However, when you set the trick up for your friends, place the cups exactly the opposite way round, with the middle cup upside down and the other two the right way up.

4 From this position it is impossible. After watching them try, reset the cups (with the middle cup the right way up) and show them how easy it is!

A cup CON-TRICK!

Sweet Surrender

This game might prove whether you are going to end up running a successful used-car business when you grow up! Can you convince your friend that they are getting a good deal when really they are losing out?

The preparation

You will need
....
A handful of candies (sweets)

A small cup or container

Share the candies equally between you and your friend.

The trick

1 Both you and your friend put two of your candies in the container.

Now ask your friend if they would like to swap the contents of the cup for three of their remaining candies. They are bound to say yes—four candies in exchange for three sounds like a bargain!

3 But you are actually one candy up on the deal. How is that?

A CONFIDENCE trick!

The secret

Your friend will have forgotten that they already put two of their candies in the container at the beginning, so in fact two of the four candies in the container already "belong" to them. They only get two of your candies for the three they have paid.

Optical Illusion

An optical illusion is something that tricks our brains into seeing things that aren't necessarily real or correct—try this simple puzzler on your friends.

The preparation

1 First trace this shape twice onto tracing paper (or thin paper that you can see through).

2 Use this pattern to draw two identical shapes onto white card. Now color in each shape in a different color—say green and pink.

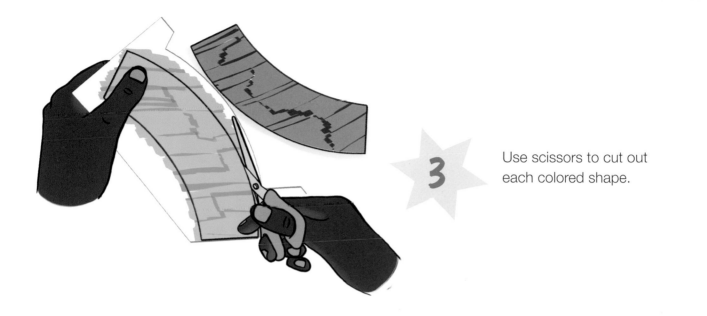

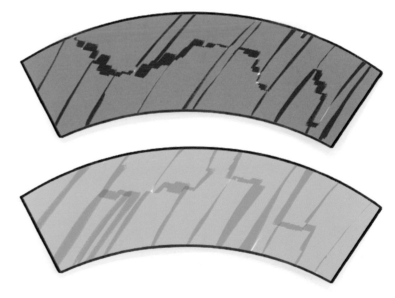

3 Use scissors to cut out each colored shape.

The trick

Lay the two colored shapes on a table so that the pink one is above the green one. Ask a friend to tell you which one is the bigger shape. Even though they are exactly the same, your friend will choose the green one. You have created an optical illusion, as the green one appears much larger than the pink. Now change them around and have the green one on top. This time the pink one is bigger. How can that be?

CONFUSE your brain!

A Knotty Problem

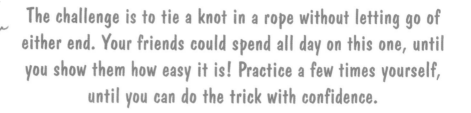

The challenge is to tie a knot in a rope without letting go of either end. Your friends could spend all day on this one, until you show them how easy it is! Practice a few times yourself, until you can do the trick with confidence.

The trick

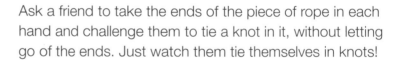

You will need

A length of rope or string, or a long shoelace

1

Ask a friend to take the ends of the piece of rope in each hand and challenge them to tie a knot in it, without letting go of the ends. Just watch them tie themselves in knots!

2

Now it's time to show them how it's done. Lay the rope down on the table in front of you and cross your arms. Make sure one hand is over the top of the opposite arm and one hand right underneath the opposite arm.

3 Without uncrossing your arms, pick up the left-hand end of the rope with your right hand, and the right-hand end of the rope with your left hand.

4 Once you have both ends in your hands, simply uncross your arms and pull the rope through the loop that will form, until a knot is tied.

The secret

By folding your arms you have actually tied a knot in your arms. This is then transferred to the rope as you uncross your arms.

Tie YOURSELF in knots!

Hat Trick

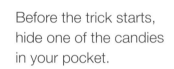

This is a great trick to play on one of your friends when you have a packet of candies (sweets); but be generous at the end and let them have one or two. You don't want to spoil a beautiful friendship!

You will need

Several identical candies (sweets)

A hat

The preparation

Before the trick starts, hide one of the candies in your pocket.

The trick

1 In full view of your friend, place the second candy under the hat.

2 Bet your friend that you can eat the candy that is covered by the hat, without even touching the hat. Put down a few more candies on the table. Tell your friend that if you can do it, you will keep all the candies, but if you can't, they can have them all. Because the trick sounds impossible your friend will almost certainly have a bet with you!

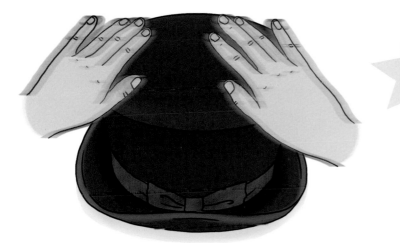

3 Wave your hands over the hat in a magical way, explaining that the candy has now vanished from under the hat.

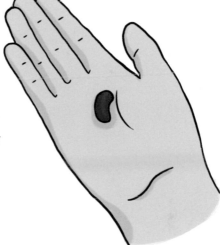

4 Take the hidden candy out of your pocket and show it to your friend, telling them it's the candy from under the hat.

5 Of course your friend won't believe you, and will immediately pick up the hat, at which point you can pick up and eat the candy that is under it. Now explain that you have won the bet. You have eaten the candy without touching the hat! Scoop up the rest of the sweets as your friend groans at having been tricked.

WON, fair and square!

Turning Hands

This "betcha" is very simple to do—and it will have your friends kicking themselves! Bet your friends that you can get them to turn their hands over, without even touching them. They'll think it's impossible—unless there is some trick involved.

The trick

1 Ask your friends to put their hands straight out in front of them.

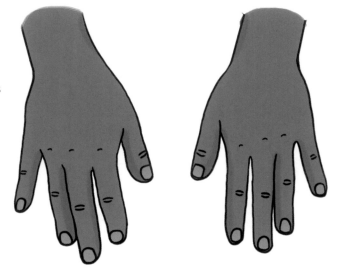

2 Whichever way their hands are, palms facing up or palms facing down, immediately say "No, the other way up."

3 As they turn their hands over, you've got them! You did exactly what you said you would do—made them turn their hands over without touching them. You win the bet!

WHO will fall for this one?

Flexible Feat

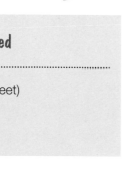

Challenge your most flexible friend to pick up a candy without bending their knees. If they can do it, they can have the candy!

The trick

You will need

1 candy (sweet)

1 Ask a friend to stand against a wall with their heels and bottom touching the wall itself.

2 Place a candy on the floor in front of them, approximately 4 in. (10 cm) in front of their toes.

3 Now set the challenge! Ask your friend to pick up the sweet by bending down (not sideways), without bending their knees. It looks easy but in fact it's impossible to do without losing your balance!

4 Now it's your turn to demonstrate how it's done. Stand in exactly the same way as they did, but just in front of an open door. That way, when you bend over you can stick your bottom out, while still keeping your legs straight. This will counterbalance the top half of your body bending forward.

The secret

This trick is all about keeping your center of gravity above your feet. Move it forward and you topple over.

Crazy Loops

☺ ☺ ○

Can you get your head through this loop of paper? What about your shoulders? Can you get your whole body through? The answer is "yes" if you know how!

The trick

You will need

A sheet of paper 20 in. (50 cm) long—newspaper will do

Scissors

Sticky tape

1 Cut a piece of paper into a long strip, approximately 24 in. (60 cm) long and 3 in. (8 cm) wide. Hold it up to show your friend. Tell them you are going to make it into a loop and challenge them to get their whole body through the loop.

2 Make one twist in the paper and then use sticky tape to stick it together to form a loop.

3 Give the loop to your friend and ask them to pull it right over their body. They won't fit! If they tear the loop, just make another one.

4

Now tell them that it can be done—you just need to snip the loop in two. Fold a small section of the loop and make a snip in the middle of the paper to get your scissors into, and then cut all along the length of the loop, right down the middle.

5

Your friend will think you will end up with two loops. They will be wrong! Because of the clever twist in the paper, you'll actually end up with one big loop. Put it over your head and step right through!

Loop the LOOP!

Full, Empty, Full, Empty

Your friends will be puzzling for a while over this one—until you show them how easy it is!

The preparation

Fill three of the glasses with water and arrange them in a line so that the first, third, and fifth glasses are full—full, empty, full, empty, full, empty.

You will need

....

6 glasses or plastic cups
Water

The trick

1 Ask your friend to move just one of the glasses so that the order is now full, full, full, empty, empty, empty.

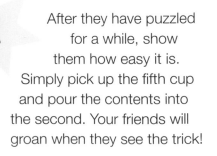

2 After they have puzzled for a while, show them how easy it is. Simply pick up the fifth cup and pour the contents into the second. Your friends will groan when they see the trick!

If I take off my shoes

This sounds like a particularly acrobatic challenge,
but it's just about outsmarting your friends!

The trick

You will need

2 small tables
Your shoes

 **1** Challenge your friend by saying "I bet if I take off my shoes and push these two tables together I can jump over them without even taking a run-up."

2 They won't believe it's possible— how can you jump over the tables? But here's the trick.

3 Take off your shoes, push the two tables together, and then jump over your shoes.

Tricked YOU!

Mirror Image

Your friends will think this is an easy "betcha" to take on—all they have to do is copy your moves exactly.

The trick

You will need

2 identical cups

Some water

1

Put a little water in the bottom of the two cups.

2

Explain to your friend that all they have to do is copy your moves, as if they were a "mirror image" of you. To make things easier, they can even delay their moves by a second or two.

3

Now give them a series of challenges to copy.
For example:
Move the cup to the left.
Move the cup back to the center.
Cough.
Take a sip of water.
Scratch your chin.
Say "Hallelujah!"

4 The next move (which you must do) is to gulp the rest of your water, but don't swallow it! Hold the water in your mouth and just let your friend think you have swallowed it.

5 Continue with a few more moves. For example:
Move the cup to the right.
Move the cup back to the center.
Scratch your right ear.

6 Now comes the trick. Hold the cup under your chin and spit the water back into your cup! Of course your friend won't be able to copy this move, as they will have already swallowed the water!

Mirror, MIRROR on the wall

chapter 4
Money tricks

Cash Cup

It's worth keeping a foreign banknote, left over from a vacation, in your magic box especially for this trick. If you don't have one of these and are down to your last few coins, you will have to borrow a banknote from an adult. Even Monopoly money would do!

You will need

A banknote

A cup full of water or juice

The trick

1 Place the cup of water on top of the banknote. Place it closer to one end rather than right in the middle.

2 Ask your friends if they believe you can remove the banknote from under the cup without touching the cup or spilling any of the liquid. Impossible, isn't it?

3 Of course it's possible—if you know the secret! Simply roll the banknote into a tube, starting at the end farthest from the cup. Keep rolling tightly, making sure you don't touch the cup with your fingers.

4

Keep rolling until the note has been completely rolled up from under the cup—you win the bet!

Roll up! **ROLL UP!**

Vanishing Coin

Show your friends that you can magically make a coin disappear. This trick needs a little preparation, but it is easy and very convincing.

The preparation

You will need

A transparent plastic cup or old glass tumbler

2 sheets of colored card

A pencil

Scissors

Glue stick

A coin

A cloth or scarf

1 Take the plastic cup and place it on top of one of the sheets of colored card. Draw around it with the pencil.

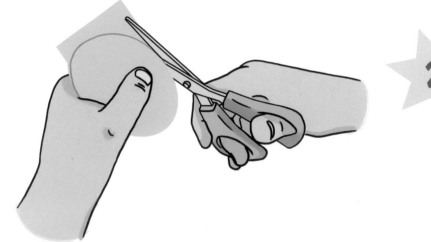

2 Cut out the circle you have drawn with a pair of scissors. You must cut it out exactly on the line.

3 Spread some glue around the rim of the cup or glass and then stick your cut-out circle onto the bottom of the cup. Be sure that no card shows outside the rim of the cup.

4 Take the other piece of colored card (it must be the same color) and place it on the table in front of you. Place the cup on top of the card. No one will be able to see the card that is stuck on the cup.

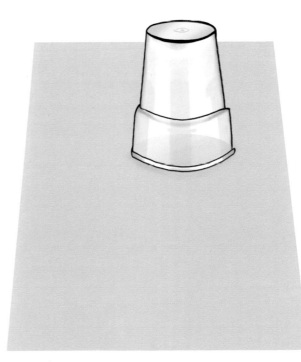

The trick

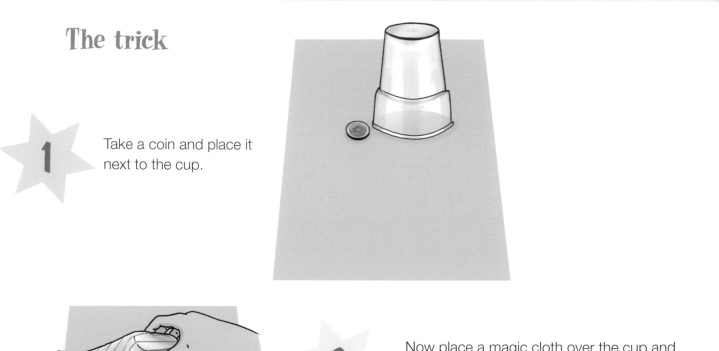

1 Take a coin and place it next to the cup.

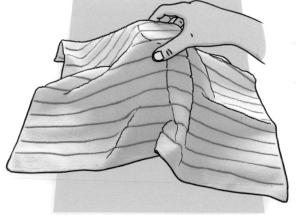

2 Now place a magic cloth over the cup and coin—your cloth should be quite big so it trails on the table around the glass. With your hand on top of the cloth, lift the cup over the coin. Say a few magic words!

3 Lift off the cloth; the coin will appear to have vanished! It is invisible beneath the stuck-on circle of card.

Now you SEE it, now you DON'T!

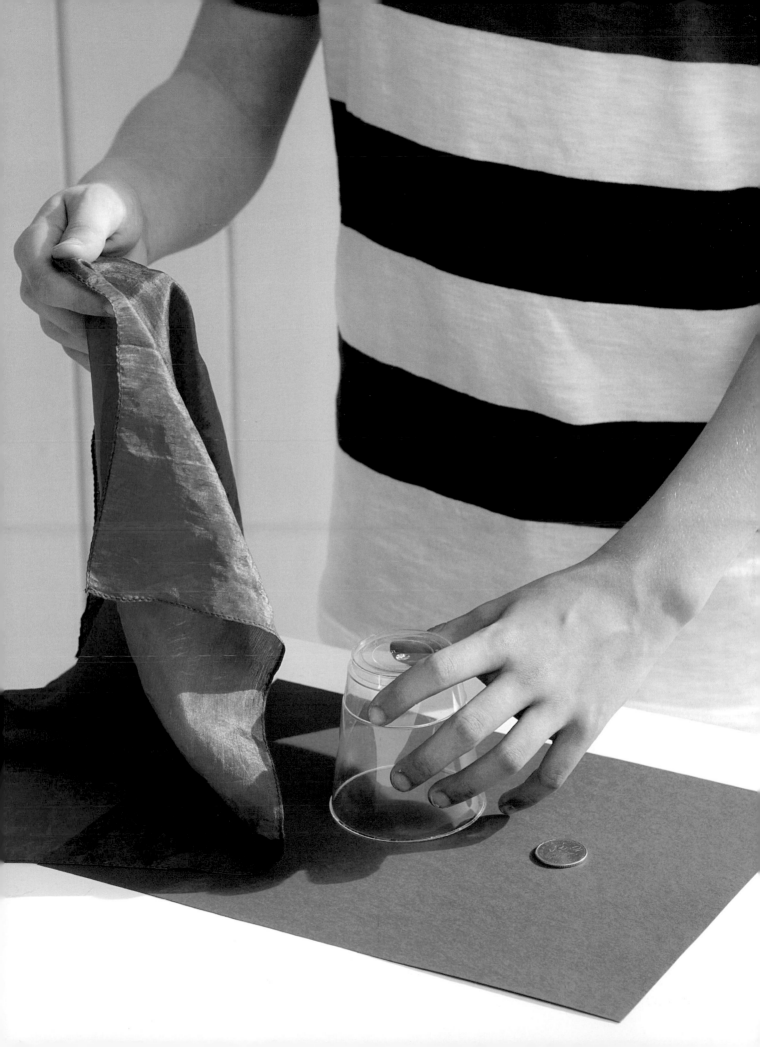

Coin Under Hanky

All magic depends on you tricking your audience in some way. This one uses an innocent-looking assistant to make a coin disappear!

The preparation

Before you start this trick, you will need to ask a friend or family member to help you perform it—your grandma is ideal, as no one will suspect her of cheating! Explain the trick and tell your helper that when it is their turn to feel the coin, they need to take it out secretly and hide it.

You will need

....

A partner

A coin

A hanky or cloth

The trick

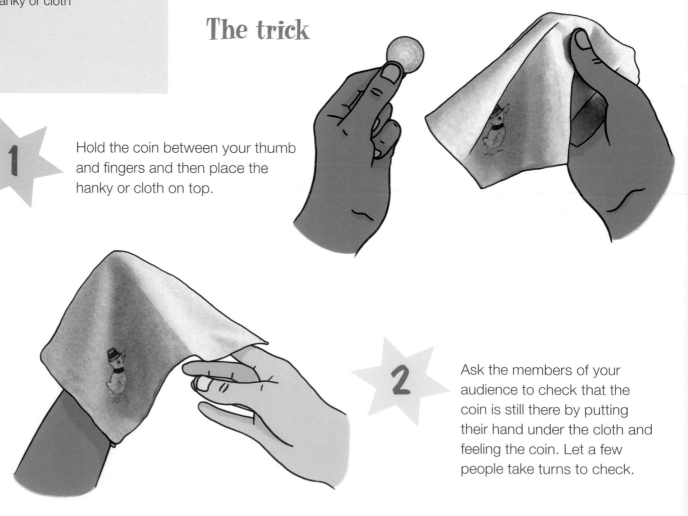

1 Hold the coin between your thumb and fingers and then place the hanky or cloth on top.

2 Ask the members of your audience to check that the coin is still there by putting their hand under the cloth and feeling the coin. Let a few people take turns to check.

3 Now ask Grandma (or whoever is your partner in crime) to feel the coin. They must feel it and then secretly take it and hide it. Keep talking to your audience to distract them from what your helper is doing.

4 A few moments later, click the fingers of your other hand, say some magic words, and remove the cloth. The coin will have vanished!

The **MAGIC** touch

Push the Coin

This is one of those tricks that is all about a play on words—
another one to make your friends groan!

The preparation

Use a pencil to draw around the smaller coin in the center of the card. Pierce the center of the circle with the point of the scissors and then cut neatly around the edge of the circle to make a small, round hole.

You will need

2 coins, one smaller than the other

A pencil

A small piece of card

Pointed scissors

The trick

1 Show the card and larger coin to a friend. Challenge them to "push the coin through the hole," without tearing or damaging the card itself.

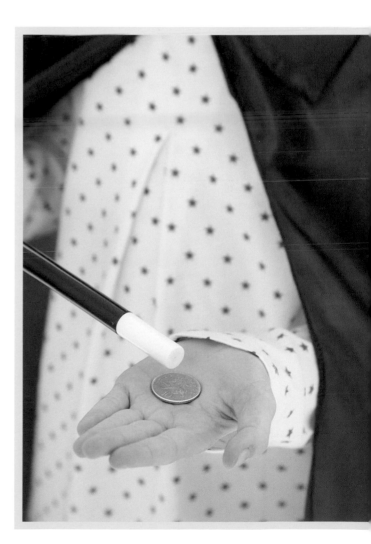

2 Try as they might, they will find it's impossible until you tell them the secret! To show them how it's done, first poke a finger through the hole in the card.

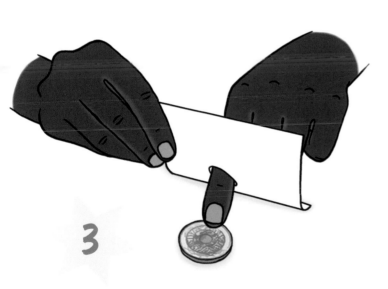

3

Now push the coin along the table with the same finger. You are pushing the coin "through the hole!"

SNEAKY, isn't it?

Melting Coin

Explain that with your "magical" powers, you can make a coin "melt away" simply by rubbing it against your elbow. This trick is all about good acting.

The trick

You will need

A coin

1

Show the coin to your audience and then rub it a few times on your elbow—remember to perform as if you are a magician!

2

While you are rubbing the coin, accidentally (on purpose) drop it on the floor. When you go to pick it up, make sure your foot is positioned near the coin.

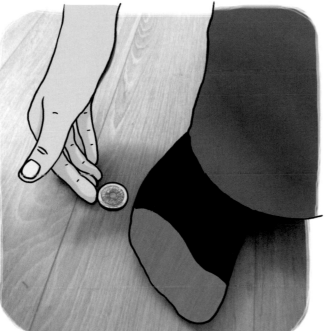

3 Now, instead of picking up the coin, you simply flick it under your foot and stand on top of it, while pretending to pick up the coin.

4 Now continue with the trick, pretending to rub the coin (which is actually under your shoe) into your elbow. Keep rubbing and then reveal that the coin has melted away!

Magical MELTING coin!

chapter 5
Mind tricks

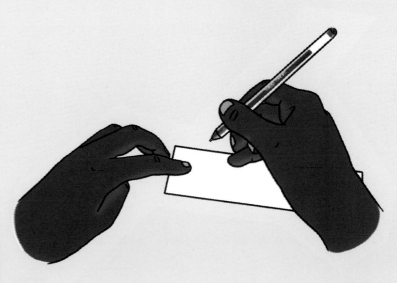

Black Magic

You will need an accomplice for this trick—explain to your audience that just using the power of the mind, your friend will be able to tell which object has been chosen by the audience.

You will need

....

A tray

A selection of objects, including one that is black

The preparation

Put together a tray of objects, making sure that one of them is black. For example, you could have a pencil, a cup, a toy, a pair of scissors—anything! Next, explain to your accomplice that you will point to the black object just before pointing to the chosen object.

The trick

1 Get your accomplice to leave the room and then ask someone in your audience to choose a random object from the tray in front of you.

2 Ask your accomplice to come back into the room. Look into their eyes for a few seconds, pretending to mind-read. Now point to various objects, asking whether each is the one that was chosen.

3 For the first few objects you point to, your accomplice will answer "No!" Then point to the black object. Your accomplice will still answer "No!" but they will know that the next item you point to will be the one that was chosen. Point to the correct item and see the surprise on your friends' faces when your accomplice answers "Yes!"

Book Test

You'll need a few people to make this trick work—as well as a willing accomplice! Can you and your accomplice convince your audience that you are actually mind reading?

The preparation

Explain to your accomplice that they must act amazed and surprised as if the words written down on the paper you give them really do match the words someone else has been reading and repeating in their head. (They won't really match!)

You will need

....
A partner

A shelf of books

A pencil

Paper

At least 3 friends

The trick

1 Explain to your friends that you are going to do some mind-reading and you require complete silence and concentration. Then, ask one of your friends to choose a book at random from the shelf in front of you.

2 Ask the second friend to open it to any page they like.

3 Ask the third friend to read the first three words— without saying them out loud—over and over in their mind. To make the trick more realistic, ask them to look into your eyes as they repeat the words in their head.

4 After a few seconds, explain that they have successfully "transmitted" the words to you, and then write them down on a piece of paper. Make sure no one can see what you write – you can write down any three words you like!

5 Fold up the piece of paper and hand it to your accomplice. Then ask the third friend (who read the three words) to say their three words out loud. Your accomplice should slowly unfold the paper and gasp in amazement as they confirm that those were the three words you wrote down (which they're not).

Feel the Magic

In some tricks you can look into a friend's eyes to see the magic. In this trick, touch their jaw and feel it. It's worth practicing first with your accomplice to make sure that you know where to feel, and that they don't give the game away by chewing too enthusiastically.

You will need

A partner

1 Ask a friend to whisper a number between 1 and 10 to your accomplice, making sure that you can't hear it.

2 Explain that you will work out what the number is by using the power of touch. First put your hand on your accomplice's shoulder, while pretending to "feel" the number.

3 Next move your hand to their forehead, then their jawline. The trick is that while your hand is resting at the back of their jaw, just in front of the corner of the jawbone, your accomplice very slightly moves their jaw up and down. If they move their jaw four times, the number picked is 4.

4 After you have felt the jaw and found out the number, move your hand onto your accomplice's nose for a few seconds, so your friend doesn't guess the trick. Only then, to the amazement of your friend, announce the secret number.

The power of TOUCH

Mind-reading Crayons

As with most tricks, the key here is to distract your audience so that they don't notice what you are doing.

The trick

You will need

A box of wax crayons

1

Ask a friend to mix up all the crayons in the box so you couldn't possibly know the order of the colors.

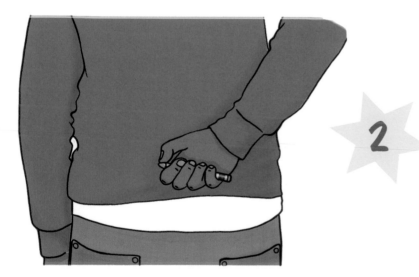

2

Now turn around, put your hand behind your back, and ask them to put any color they like into your hand. Turn round to face them.

3

Here's the trick! While you are holding the crayon, use your thumbnail to scrape the crayon a little—this is done behind your back so no one will be able to see.

4 After a few seconds, ask them to take the crayon back and to place it in the box without you seeing what it was. Again, ask them to mix the crayons around so the colors are jumbled up. While they are doing this, take a quick glance at your thumbnail so you can see which color you were holding.

5 Now for the mind-reading! Ask them to concentrate on the chosen color while you stare into their eyes.

6 Act as if you have suddenly "read" the color in your friend's eyes and pick up the box of crayons. Take out the crayons, one by one, until you find the crayon you were holding. Announce that that is the one!

COLOR magic!

The gray elephant from Denmark

You'll only be able to play this trick on your friend once, as they'll soon realize that there is only one answer!

The trick

1 Ask a friend to think of a number between 2 and 9, without telling you what it is. Tell them to multiply that number by 9.

$3 \times 9 = 63$

$6 + 3 = 9$

2 They will now have a new two-digit number. Ask them to add those two digits together.

1=A 2=B
3=C 4=D 5=E

3 Now ask them to take 5 away from their new number. In this case, the answer will be 4. Tell them to turn their number into a letter using the code: 1 = A, 2 = B, 3 = C, 4 = D, 5 = E, and so on.

4 Without telling you what it is, ask them to think of a country that begins with their letter (in this case "D").

5 Now ask them to think of an animal (not a bird or a fish) that begins with the second letter of the country they just thought of—again without telling you.

6 Next, ask them to think of the usual color of their chosen animal. So now they should have thought of a color, an animal, and a country.

7 At this point it's time for you to guess these three "random" words… is it a gray elephant from Denmark?

The secret

The trick here is making your friend think they are making their own choice, when in fact they will always come up with the same answer. When you multiply any number between 2 and 9 by 9, the two digits of the answer will always add up to 9 (helpful when learning your 9 times table!) So the letter in step 4 will always be "D," and there are very few countries that begin with the letter "D." And if you ask someone to think quickly of an animal that begins with the letter "E," most everyone will think of the same large gray elephant!

chapter 6
Pranks

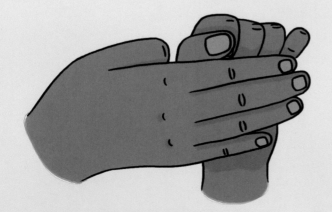

The Sneeze

This is a really gross trick—which is why you'll love it so much!

1 Give your hands a good wash, but don't dry them.

2 Sneak up behind your friend and pretend to sneeze loudly.

3 As you make your sneezing sound, shake your hands, flicking water onto the back of your friend's neck. They will think (for a moment) that you have just sneezed snot all over them! Yuck!

How **DISGUSTING!**

Cracking Nose

Explain to your friends that your nose is broken, and if they listen carefully they will be able to hear the bones cracking. Any squeamish friends will run screaming from the room!

1 Place your hands over your nose.

2 Make sure your thumbnails are resting under your top front teeth.

3 Now push your nose from side to side while at the same time flicking your thumbnails against your front teeth to make a clicking sound.

The secret

You will have to practice this in front of a mirror so that you can do it without revealing the trick.

Bone-clickingly funny!

Don't Say 17

This is another trick that will make your friends hopping mad.

1 Challenge a friend not to say the number 17 while you time them for one minute. The rules are that they have to answer your questions, without saying the number 17. If they say it, they've lost!

You will need

....

A stopwatch

2 Start a stopwatch and ask them the following questions:
What's 10 + 10?
What's 20 + 10?
What's 30 + 10?
What's 40 + 10?
What's 50 + 10?
What's 60 + 9?
What's 69 + 1?

3 When they give the final answer, "70," shrug your shoulders and tell them they have lost. They will immediately protest and say that you told them not to say "17," not "70."

4 Now you can stop the clock and explain that this time they really have lost as they have just said "17!" You have won the challenge!

Some tricky SUMS

Magic Pen

The magic pen won't produce bunny rabbits out of a hat or turn you into a frog, but it can write in any color you like!

You will need

An ordinary black pen

A sheet of paper

1 Ask a friend to put your "magic" pen to the test by naming any color (for example, yellow).

2 Now show them the magic! Simply spell out the color they named, writing each letter clearly in black ink!

Money Worries

Here's a way to entertain your friends with just a coin—but it will be difficult if you bite your nails!

You will need

....

A coin

1

Start by pressing a coin into your forehead for about 10 seconds. When you take your hand away, it will stick to your head.

2

With your hands behind your back, show your friends how to release the coin simply by frowning. The coin will drop off as you wrinkle your forehead.

3

Now get a friend to try. However, you must be the one to press the coin onto their forehead. As you press, make sure that one of your fingernails is just under the edge of the coin. This will stop it sticking to their skin.

4 After 10 seconds, lift the coin away, pretending that you are just taking away your hand.

5 Your friend will feel as if the coin is still stuck to their forehead. Now you can have lots of fun watching them frown and pull ridiculous faces to try and remove it.

Frantic FROWNS!

Removable Thumb

You don't need any props for this one—just your two hands, a bendy right thumb, and a friend to trick!

The preparation

 **1** Hold your right hand in front of you as shown.

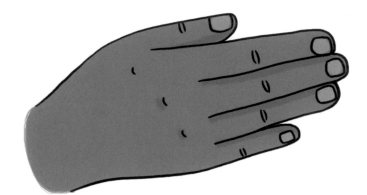

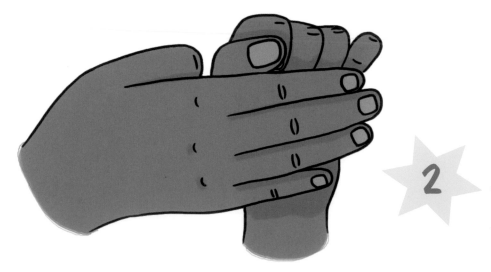

2 Bend your right thumb and then place the thumb of your left hand into the position that your right thumb would normally occupy.

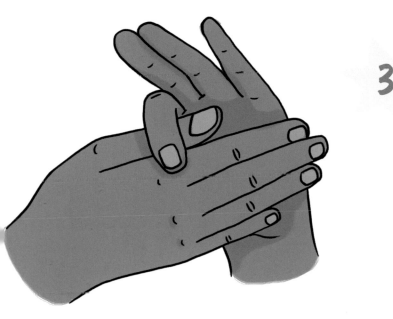

3 Cover up the join with the first finger of your left hand.

Not for the SQUEAMISH!

The trick

Once you have your fingers in position, you are ready to scare your friends! Slide your left hand along your right fingers—it will look as if you are removing your right thumb!

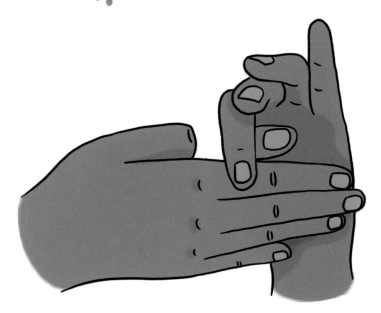

Target Practice

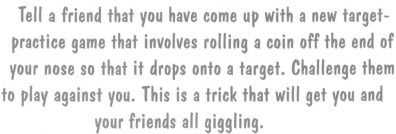

Tell a friend that you have come up with a new target-practice game that involves rolling a coin off the end of your nose so that it drops onto a target. Challenge them to play against you. This is a trick that will get you and your friends all giggling.

The preparation

You will need

....

A sheet of letter (A4) paper

A graphite pencil

Some round objects to draw around

A coin with a grooved edge

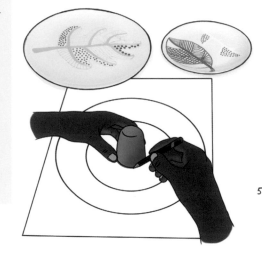

1 Start by drawing a target on your sheet of paper —you need three circles, so use three objects to draw around such as a plate, a saucer, and an eggcup. Write in the numbers that will give the scores.

5 10 25 50 25 10 5

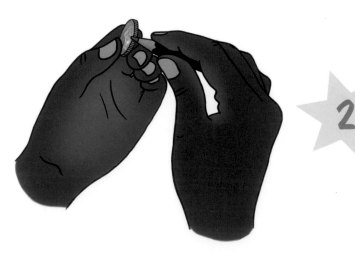

2 Take your coin and rub all around the edge with the side of your pencil lead. Make sure that you leave plenty of graphite from the pencil in the grooves of the coin.

The trick

1 Say that you will go first to show your friend what to do. Roll the coin down your face from your forehead until it reaches the end of your nose, then drop it onto the target, which is on the table below you—BUT don't let the coin actually touch your face, just make it look as if you are rolling it—this takes a bit of practice!

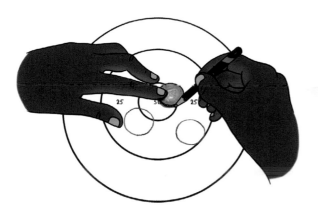

2 Wherever the coin lands, draw around it and write in the score. As you draw round it, rub plenty more graphite onto the edge of the coin. Have five goes, add up your scores, and then let your friend have a turn.

3 Of course, when your friend rolls the coin, they will really touch their face and the graphite will make a neat grey trail all the way down their nose. If they do it five times, they will have five gray lines! Try not to giggle and don't tell them what has happened—someone else soon will!

Never-ending Thread

Eagle-eyed friends won't fail to notice that a loose thread is hanging from your jacket—but what happens when they try to remove it?

The preparation

1 Pull some thread off the spool and thread a needle onto the end, keeping the thread attached to the spool.

You will need

A small spool of thread (reel of cotton)

Needle

A loose jacket (one with an inside pocket is best)

2 Push the needle through the front of your jacket, from inside to outside.

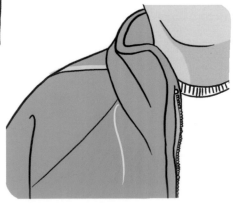

3 Remove the needle so it looks as if you have a loose thread on your clothes—you only need to pull through just enough thread to be noticed.

4 Tuck the spool of thread inside your jacket, out of sight.

The trick

Now wait for someone to notice the thread and "helpfully" remove it. Watch their surprise as the thread just keeps on going and going!

When will it STOP?

Index

To find out more about Paul Megram please visit:
www.paulmegram.com and
www.colonelcustard.com